STRESS
FREE
LIVING

STRESS FREE LIVING

GUILLERMO MALDONADO

WHITAKER
HOUSE

ERJ Publications credits:
Editor: Jose Anhuaman
Editorial development: Gloria Zura
Cover design: Danielle Cruz-Nieri

STRESS-FREE LIVING

Guillermo Maldonado • 14100 SW 144th Ave. • Miami, FL 33186
King Jesus Ministry / ERJ Publications
www.kingjesus.org / www.ERJPub.org

ISBN: 978-1-64123-335-4 • eBook ISBN: 978-1-64123-336-1
Printed in the United States of America • © 2019 by Guillermo Maldonado

Whitaker House • 1030 Hunt Valley Circle • New Kensington, PA 15068
www.whitakerhouse.com

Library of Congress Cataloging-in-Publication Data (pending)

1 2 3 4 5 6 7 8 9 10 11 **WH** 26 25 24 23 22 21 20 19

CONTENTS

FOREWORD

I met Apostle Guillermo Maldonado of King Jesus Ministry while we were both attending an event in Washington, D.C. You could say that we met by coincidence, but I think it was more than that. I believe God's hand was in it. He and I immediately hit it off. We share the same passion: to guide people to wholeness in their lives physically, emotionally, mentally, and spiritually. When we met, I told him how I felt a call to bring health and healing to men and women who are serving God. Since then, I have developed a close friendship with Apostle Maldonado, as well as a professional relationship with him as his doctor. I regularly speak at events at King Jesus Ministry on healing, health, and nutrition, and I give his books to my patients.

As a medical doctor who digs deeply into the original causes of illness, as well as the underlying elements that promote health, I know of a variety of factors that either influence the development of disease or support our overall well-being. I am not only referring to what might strictly be termed "medicine," but also to elements such as diet, hormones, toxins, emotions, thinking patterns, and much more. I can affirm from both personal and professional experience that the potent effect of negative stress is one of those influences that has a significant impact on our health.

In my book *Stress Less*, I define stress as "the pressures of life and how one perceives, believes, reacts, and copes with these pressures." As Apostle Maldonado points out, prolonged stress in a person's life can lead to a number of serious illnesses, the interruption of normal daily living, estrangement from others, and additional problems. While there are various elements that contribute to stress, it is easy to latch on to one or two of those elements and ignore other factors that contribute equally or perhaps to an even greater extent. While physical, emotional, and mental elements all play a part, in my decades of exploration into healthy living, I have always recognized the central role of the spiritual component in our lives. This is an area that some people ignore or dismiss. But we have a Creator who loves us and wants the best for us in all aspects of our lives, and He offers us wisdom in His Word and spiritual power to address our problems and concerns. There are some issues that only the intervention of God can overcome.

Apostle Maldonado has seen the destructive toll of stress on people in America and around the world. *Stress-Free Living* is based on his years of experience in helping people to be released from stress and its devastating effects. It includes first-hand accounts of those who have overcome the oppression of stress through his ministry. This book will help you to identify the factors that contribute to your stress—especially entrenched cycles of stress that are controlling your life and robbing you of inner peace, strong relationships, and fruitful living.

Most important, you will not just find a quick fix to help you through today's anxiety, fear, or depression—you will find answers to achieving long-lasting relief from stress through the wisdom and power of God.

—*Don Colbert, M.D.*
Best-selling author of over forty books, including *Stress Less*, *The 7 Pillars of Health*, *Eat This and Live!*, *The Bible Cure for AutoImmune Diseases*, and *What Would Jesus Eat?*

A STRESSFUL WORLD

A recent Gallup poll found that more than a third of the world's population experiences a lot of worry and stress. Stress is having such a negative effect in the U.S., where nearly half of Americans say they're suffering from it, that it's eating away at their overall well-being, according to the American Psychological Association.[1]

---

1. Maggie Fox, "The World Is Significantly Unhappier, Gallup Poll Finds," *Today* show, September 12, 2018, https://www.today.com/health/americans-world-feel-more-stress-less-happiness-t137282. Christopher Bergland, "Stress in America Is Gnawing Away at Our Overall Well-Being," *The Athlete's Way* blog, *Psychology Today*, November 1, 2017, https://www.psychologytoday.com/us/blog/the-athletes-way/201711/stress-in-america-is-gnawing-away-our-overall-well-being. See also https://www.apa.org/news/press/releases/stress/2017/state-nation.pdf.

In one way or another, all of us experience stress—regardless of our age, race, gender, social standing, or financial status.

We live in an agitated world, and many people find themselves constantly running against the clock, struggling to keep up with responsibilities and trying to make ends meet. Often, we find ourselves needing to make key decisions that affect our lives and those of our family members. All these factors can contribute to mental and emotional stress. In addition, on television and the Internet, we are bombarded by news about crises in our country and around the world: natural disasters, wars, hunger, misery, economic failures, political discord, crime, societal breakdown, environmental worries, and more.

Our world is full of stress. Our lives are full of stress. These are the times we're living in.

> *Experiencing ongoing stress takes a tremendous toll on us.*

Yet experiencing ongoing stress takes a tremendous toll. Many people deal with constant anxiety or fear. Others struggle with deeper issues of anguish and oppression. Depending on its degree, stress can be uncomfortable, life-disrupting— or life-threatening. According to the American Psychological

Association, "Chronic stress is linked to the six leading causes of death: heart disease, cancer, lung ailments, accidents, cirrhosis of the liver and suicide. And more than 75 percent of all physician office visits are for stress-related ailments and complaints."[2]

WHAT IS STRESS?

You have probably picked up this book because you or a loved one is affected by some level of stress. I felt an urgency to write *Stress-Free Living* to help people address the destructive effects of stress—its causes and consequences physically, emotionally, mentally, and spiritually. I want to demonstrate that you can experience relief, hope, and joy, no matter what level of stress you are dealing with. Together, we will discover the underlying causes of stress, how to keep it from getting a grip on your life, and how to live free of stress.

Generally speaking, stress is a state of alertness, anxiety, or fear. However, the first thing we must understand is that stress itself is not always negative. In its basic form, it is a built-in physiological response that is triggered in emergency situations when we believe we are facing a threat or danger, whether real or perceived, or during times when we experience heightened expectations for performance regarding a particular task, whether the expectations are self-generated or come from an outside source.

2. Deborah S. Hartz-Seeley, "Chronic Stress Is Linked to the Six Leading Causes of Death," *Miami Herald*, March 21, 2014, https://www.miamiherald.com/living/article1961770.html.

How does the body react to stress? It releases hormones, such as adrenaline, as a "survival mechanism." Adrenaline accelerates the heartbeat, raises blood pressure, tenses muscles, increases blood flow to the large muscles, produces sweat, reduces pain, and generates other effects. When we face danger, a short-term stress response can save our lives by enabling us to take immediate and effective action. However, if we remain in an ongoing state of stress, then physical, mental, emotional, and spiritual damage can occur. Our mind and body become overloaded, causing us to pay a high price, whether in the short run or the long run.

What this means is that, in a temporary form, in situations such as those described above, stress can help us to function quickly under pressure and motivate us to give the best of ourselves. But when such stress reaction is prolonged, it can be extremely harmful to us. Our body, mind, and emotions are not designed to live perpetually in an emergency state.

*If you surrender continuously to stress,
it will enslave you.*

Whatever people constantly tolerate or consent to becomes their norm. That is why, if we give in to anxiety or fear in our lives, it will begin to define us. This is the point where stress is not just something we experience from time to time in certain circumstances, but has developed into something that has taken hold of us. When this occurs, we are dealing with spiritual factors as well as physical and emotional ones. Many people don't recognize this spiritual element to their stress, and that is why they remain in its grip.

TWO TYPES OF STRESS

For the purposes of this book, we will define stress in two ways: natural stress and spiritual stress.

Natural Stress

Natural stress remains largely in the physical, emotional, and mental spheres, although spiritual elements can influence it. There are various causes of stress, and we will cover a number of them in chapter 2. Natural stress can produce physical symptoms such as headaches, neck and shoulder tension, back pain, fatigue, stomach problems, sleeplessness, and severe skin irritation. It can also produce emotional and mental symptoms, such as anxiety, deep sadness, anger, impatience, irritability, feelings of hopelessness, trouble concentrating, a certain degree of memory loss, and negative thoughts. Although we might temporarily feel stress when we are placed in new situations or are challenged to meet high expectations, in many cases, stress manifests as a result of upsetting situations we are exposed to over time.

Spiritual Stress

When stress is in a natural stage, an individual has the ability to learn to manage and control it. However, when it has entered the spiritual stage, it cannot be controlled using natural methods, and therefore significant spiritual issues must be addressed.

With spiritual stress, there are several types of controlling "yokes" that can manifest, such as jealousy, fear, anger, and depression. For example, when a person crosses over from feeling under pressure regarding a situation to living in a state of depression, they become imprisoned in despair. The yoke of stress shapes or molds them into certain ways of thinking, which are reflected in their behavior. When someone falls into depression, their very countenance changes. Their features may droop or become hard. Some people move into a self-destructive mode as their depression dulls their ability to function normally. Among the symptoms of depression are deep and continuous sadness, feelings of hopelessness, low self-esteem, pessimism, guilt, physical pain, digestive problems, changes in sleep patterns and appetite, abuse of alcohol or drugs, illicit sex, gambling, and thoughts of suicide.

When we live in depression, we have no expectation of anything good, and we cannot see a way out of our problems—even at times when a challenge may be relatively easy to overcome.

The Bible provides several examples of people who suffered from depression as a result of stress. I believe that the great leader and lawmaker Moses fell into depression, and it kept him from entering into the promised land even after he had freed God's people from Egyptian slavery. It was what ultimately ended his leadership. For years, Moses had been accumulating all the burdens of his people in his heart, until he became exhausted and depressed. Because he was angry about the people's continual rebellion, complaints, and disbelief, he disobeyed God in a major way. (See Numbers 20:8–13.) As expressed above, when we struggle with depression, we may behave in self-destructive ways—which we will later regret.

> *When stress enters the oppressive stage, it cannot be controlled through natural means; it must be addressed spiritually.*

In another example, Elijah was one of the greatest prophets of the Old Testament. In faith, he boldly defeated four hundred and fifty prophets of the false god Baal in the power of the living God. However, when he was threatened with death by Queen Jezebel, he became afraid and chose to flee. After a while, he lost all hope and fell into a state of depression; he was spiritually oppressed, to the point of wanting to die. But Elijah was ultimately restored by rest, nutrition, encouraging words from God, spiritual strengthening, and renewed faith. His story gives us a preview of how we, too, can overcome stress that comes from fear, fatigue, and lost hope. (See 1 Kings 18:20–40; 19:1–18.)

If we are in a state of advanced stress, but do not understand what has us bound, we will not recognize that we are being oppressed by an outside force and not just our own inward struggles. Only the power of God can free us from such a tyrannical influence. The Bible teaches us, *"Do not give the devil a foothold"* (Ephesians 4:27 NIV). When we allow the devil—the evil spiritual being that opposes God—to gain a foothold in our lives through a prolonged period of stress in which we hold on to fear, anxiety, anger, or hopelessness, we will become oppressed.

God has more than enough power to break the tyranny of stress and remove every burden from us.

However, we can be assured that no matter what type of yoke comes upon us through stress, God has more than enough power to break it and remove every burden from us. We have this assurance from the Scriptures: *"It shall come to pass in that day that his burden will be taken away from your shoulder, and his yoke from your neck, and the yoke will be destroyed because of the anointing oil"* (Isaiah 10:27). Jesus Christ, God's Son, has already defeated the devil. He wants to set us free, and we can learn to live continually in His victory.

MANAGING AND DEFEATING STRESS

We must remember that when we encounter various stressful situations at home, at work, at school, and in other contexts, this is often just a natural part of living, and we can learn to manage our stress. In this book, I demonstrate how we handle these situations by looking to God's peace and strength. Beyond that, there may be other times when we sense we are holding on to stress for extended periods of time or that stress seems to have a grip on us. It is not God's will for us to live stressed, depressed, and on the verge of collapse. We need to be set free and begin to trust in the One who rules heaven and earth and can help us in our circumstances. Jesus said, *"If you can believe, all things are possible to him who believes"* (Mark 9:23), and *"These things I have spoken to you, that in Me you may have peace. In the world you will have tribulation; but be of good cheer, I have overcome the world"* (John 16:33).

If you recognize that you have some symptoms of oppressive stress, then you need the help of Jesus and the power of God's Holy Spirit. Perhaps you don't know how to pray and ask God for help. Before we move on to the next chapter, I invite you to pray the following prayer with me, knowing that if we declare it in faith, your stress can begin to change to peace, your sadness to joy, and your despair to hope. Pray believing in your heart that God will act in your life:

> Lord Jesus, I recognize that there are situations beyond my control that have robbed me of peace, bound my emotions, and caused sickness in my body. Stress has progressed into spiritual oppression and taken over. I repent for the mistakes I have made, and I ask You to forgive me for allowing stress to invade my life. Today, I need Your help to be free. I accept the forgiveness You have provided for me by Your death on the cross, when You took my sins and failings on Yourself, and by Your resurrection from the dead. I receive You into my heart, and I ask the Holy Spirit to bring peace, faith, and freedom to my mind, soul, and body. Today, in Your name, I make the decision to let go of all anxiety, sadness, worry, and everything else that causes me stress and depression. I receive peace, healing, faith, and hope from You. Thank You, Lord Jesus! Amen.

TRUE STORIES OF OVERCOMING OPPRESSIVE STRESS

Delivered from Fear

Michael has worked in law enforcement in Miami, Florida, USA, for twenty-four years, nine of those years as a police officer and fifteen as a detective. However, while he was growing up, the stress of shyness and losing his parents at a young age degenerated into a terrible fear of public speaking, until he discovered that true identity, confidence, and courage come from God the Father.

The biggest battle of my life—my biggest giant—was always fear. I was very shy from the time I was a little boy, and I was always afraid to speak in public. Then, my parents died when I was thirteen, and I became very insecure. I did not know who I was. I was always quiet and stayed away from everyone else because fear dominated me. I had a girlfriend, who is now my wife, and people always asked her why I did not speak, why I sat alone, apart, with a grim face.

My fear and insecurity caused me a lot of stress. It was exhausting! I had no peace! And I continually suffered from my fear of speaking. I was afraid that people would see that maybe I was not as educated or intelligent as I wanted them to believe. I felt I had nothing to offer.

When I joined the police force, I was terrified to speak before another officer. I did not feel smart, and that caused me stress. Today, I thank God because when I started seeking His face with all my heart and had an encounter with Him, He set me free me from that terror. As a police officer, I now face people with the courage of God. In the force, that is called "command presence"; now, I walk with that presence. My life has been transformed! I walk with the authority that God has given me as His son. I know who I am, I have an identity, and I can fulfill God's will.

Currently, I am a House of Peace[3] leader and I mentor several people. I can minister to them and speak to them with authority. When I go to work, I know that the atmosphere must change because I am a child of God and I have His authority and His power. So, I can raise my voice of command and rule from the spiritual realm. In fact, I have seen how crime has decreased in my city. Now, I am a husband, father, mentor, and leader, and I live free of stress. Fear has remained in the past. Now I see the glory of God with every step I take!

---

3. A House of Peace refers to the home of a member of King Jesus International Ministry who opens his or her door to receive neighbors, relatives, and friends with the purpose of sharing the gospel of God's kingdom—teaching the Word of God and imparting His power.

Freed from Depression

Aretha had spent her entire life dealing with depression, which she thought she had under control by taking pills. During a time of great stress, due to excessive work and studies, she had a crisis and the medications began to produce adverse side effects that were difficult to manage.

Ever since I was in high school, I had struggled with depression. I felt so much pressure and stress from my studies that I started having depressive thoughts. The psychologists wanted to give me medicine, but I refused to take it. Later, after graduating as a nurse, I was talking about prayer at work, and a patient was listening to me from the other side of the curtain in her hospital room. This patient was having surgery, and when it came time for me to interview her before the surgery, she gave me a small, blue book entitled *Power and Authority to Destroy the Works of the Devil* by Guillermo Maldonado. She told me, "I want to read it, but I feel I should give it to you."

I took the book and put it on a small table next to my bed. It sat there for almost a year, because I was "very busy." Last year, I was under a lot of stress because, in addition to working two jobs, I was getting my master's degree. I started having suicidal thoughts. That scared me! I called a nurse friend of mine and asked her if I could be prescribed antidepressants. I did not tell her that I wanted to kill myself; I did not want to worry anyone. She told me it would take a month for the medicine to have an effect, but it only took six days. I felt that I was flying! I had so much energy. I had found my cure, but I had a lot of insomnia.

One day, around three o'clock in the morning, awake and regretting the effects of the medication, I prayed to God, saying, "Lord, look at all these side effects; I'm so sensitive. What else is going to happen to me? Though I do not want to stop taking the medicine, I need to talk with You." Then, I began to read the book the patient had given me as a gift. In a very small paragraph, the author said that the Father loves His children and heals them. At that moment, I put down the book, took the medication in my hands, and said, "Lord, I have prayed for so long for You to deliver me.... At this moment, I have one thousand percent confidence in the pills. Are You telling me that You do not love me enough to heal me?" When I said that, I must have touched God's heart, because my life changed from that moment on. I have been totally free of depression for two years and I am living the best days of my life. I do not take pills and I am helping others to get out of depression.

2

CAUSES OF STRESS

At times, life can become a vicious cycle of anxiety and stress. Yet the majority of people are so immersed in their daily responsibilities that they barely have time to identify exactly what stresses them or what stresses them the most. We have seen that some causes of stress are physical or emotional, while others are entirely spiritual. We must know how to deal effectively with each, since every person and circumstance is different. Some people may have a greater capacity than others to adapt to certain situations.

What causes you stress? What is the greatest stress factor in your life? To know how to deal with your stress, you must first identify its cause. Let's look at some of the most prominent stress-inducers.

ANXIETY

Anxiety is based on uncertainty about the future. Some people are anxious and worried about what will happen to them because they feel they are not in control of their lives or a particular situation. It has been said that this generation is living in the era of anxiolytics—medications that block anxiety—because many people are resorting to medicine and treatments to control their apprehensions and worries. According to the Anxiety and Depression Association of America, "Anxiety disorders are the most common mental illness in the U.S., affecting 40 million adults in the United States age 18 and older, or 18.1% of the population every year."[4] People are anxious about the economy and being able to earn enough money to live. They are worried about their work, obtaining an education, reaching their goals, their children's future, crime in the streets, and so on. Such anxiety and worry makes them vulnerable to stress.

FEAR

In addition to anxiety, outright fear can cause people to experience the effects of stress. As we discussed in the previous chapter, many people live in fear because of distressing

---

4. See https://adaa.org/about-adaa/press-room/facts-statistics.

events and trends that are occurring in the world today. They may experience restlessness, panic attacks, and even anguish, for fear of what might happen to them, their family members, their job or business, or other concerns. More than twenty centuries ago, Jesus described such a time:

> *And there will be signs in the sun, in the moon, and in the stars; and on the earth distress of nations, with perplexity, the sea and the waves roaring; men's hearts failing them from fear and the expectation of those things which are coming on the earth, for the powers of the heavens will be shaken.*　　　　　(Luke 21:25–26)

In the above passage, the word *"perplexity"* in the original Greek essentially means "to see no way out." When we cannot seem to find a way out of a problem or situation for ourselves, our family, our finances, our work, or another area of our lives, we become distressed. Fear invades us, and we lose heart.

Stress is often based on anxiety and fear about the future.

UNREALISTIC EXPECTATIONS

Another cause of stress is when we experience a discrepancy between our expectations of a situation and the reality of that situation. To use a simple example, suppose someone plans to fly from Miami to New York on a flight that takes two and a half hours. But then, the flight is delayed, and they are informed that they will arrive in New York four hours later than they anticipated. Because the trip will take longer than they expected and their plans in New York will also be delayed, they become nervous, anxious, and irritable toward the people around them. They become stressed because they don't want to adjust their expectations to their reality.

There are many negative circumstances in life that we *can* change for the better, and we should take action to remedy them. However, if we can't change our circumstances, such as in the above example, but we still keep our original expectations, then we open the door to stress in our lives.

EXCESSIVE RESPONSIBILITIES

Many people today find themselves taking on too many responsibilities and obligations, and it becomes difficult to handle them all. Whenever they are not willing to either give up excess responsibilities or delegate them to others, this can produce chronic stress in their lives. Some people refuse to relinquish an extra job or activity because they fear a loss of prestige, income, or another benefit, even though holding on to it is costly to their mental, emotional, and spiritual health.

There are times when carrying excess responsibility can't be helped, especially during certain seasons of life. These may be temporary situations. However, overcommitment is often the result of making a bad decision or an inability to say no when people ask us to do something. If you know that you have little free time, but you continue to accept responsibilities, then you need to stop and set your priorities in order. You must decide what is most important or urgent in your life right now and focus on that, putting everything else aside.

Stress is a burden that can come upon us due to excessive responsibilities and a lack of time.

FAMILY ISSUES

Family relationships can be a major source of stress. Husbands and wives often need to navigate difficult situations and organize multiple activities within their household, especially if they have children. When they are stubborn or selfish about their own needs and wants, their relationships break down and the peace of the home is disturbed. Couples may also deal with issues like infertility, prolonged illness, the loss of loved ones, or rebellious children. They may battle over who is in charge of decision-making or argue about one spouse's seeming apathy in the relationship. If the marriage breaks up, one spouse usually has to take on the roles of both father and mother. Problems can also come from extended family members, including parents-in-law, brothers-in-law, sisters-in-law, uncles, cousins, and so forth, who try to intrude on private family matters.

Children can experience stress in the family for a variety of reasons. They may have trouble getting along with siblings. Or, their mother and father may not take on the parents' natural responsibilities in the home, so the children are forced to assume adult tasks of running the household at an early age. This can generate anxiety, insecurity, fear, resentment, or depression in young people, causing serious hindrances to their growth and development.

Such family issues, especially when they occur simultaneously, can produce significant stress in and among family members that begins to take over their lives.

WORK PRESSURES

In the business world, it is often said that "time is money." This outlook can lead employees to be placed under heavy work demands, causing them to live in continuous stress. A business owner may pressure himself and the manager of his company to produce results. In turn, the manager pressures the employees. The idea is that everyone needs to produce to the maximum, in the shortest time possible, and at the lowest costs. There are often constant and unrealistic deadlines. The hours become long, the salaries remain low, and the pressure is continual. Many people end up "living to work instead of working to live."

Additionally, in today's society, making money and spending money on consumer products and services often seem to be higher priorities than anything else. People go deeper and deeper into debt because they purchase items they can't afford. To pay off these items, they then have to work more and produce more—generating an ceaseless cycle. People's heavy work schedules is one reason why a lack of time has become one of the greatest causes of stress today.

INSUFFICIENT SLEEP

How many hours of sleep do you get on average? Research indicates that "35% of Americans don't get the recommended seven hours of sleep each night" and "three quarters of those who suffer from depression also suffer from a lack of sleep."[5] Additionally, the Centers for Disease Control and Prevention (CDC) reports, "Lack of sleep has been linked to heart disease,

---

5. "Sleep Statistics Reveal the (Shocking) Cost to Health And Society, *The Good Body*, December 10, 2018, https://www.thegoodbody.com/sleep-statistics/.

obesity, diabetes, depression, and anxiety—not to mention safety issues like drowsy driving and injuries."[6]

What are the reasons for this lack of sleep? Part of the problem is people's overcommitted, busy lives, in which they don't allow themselves a proper night's rest. But other people suffer from insomnia for mental, emotional, or physical reasons, and sleeplessness becomes a real torment to them. They know they need sleep—and their bodies know it too. However, they cannot fall asleep or stay asleep for long. Such a condition causes stress for people not only because they experience worry and fatigue, but also because they are unable to function well during the day, leading to further issues and consequences.

FINANCIAL SHORTFALLS AND CRISES

Unemployment, a lack of opportunity to develop a new business, the shaking of the global economy, recession, global indebtedness, and generational poverty can all contribute to stress. Our standard of living can be affected by any of the above, producing a state of anxiety and even despair. When people struggle financially, many begin to look for new sources of income. They may work double shifts, take a second job, or start a home-based business. They may also seek to reduce expenses or sell some of their belongings to provide for the necessities of life. While some activities such as reducing

6. "America's Most Sleep-Deprived Workers," CBS News, https://www.cbsnews.com/pictures/americas-most-sleep-deprived-workers/.

expenses or streamlining one's belongings might be helpful for anyone, the stress of trying to meet a chronic financial short-fall can be relentless, exacting a heavy personal cost.

ILLNESS IN THE FAMILY

When someone is suddenly diagnosed with a life-threatening illness, such as cancer or heart disease, the whole family is affected. The dynamics among the family members change, and all their activities begin to revolve around the ill person's health, for fear of losing them. The doctors can treat the patient's physical symptoms, although the person is often dealing with resulting mental and emotional stress as well. Additionally, when someone becomes ill, much less attention is paid to the stress suffered by the patient's relatives, who have to be strong in order to give support to their loved one. If the disease is prolonged, the stress is also prolonged, and this can affect the mental, emotional, physical, and spiritual health of all the family members.

A DEAD-END SITUATION

We have noted how fear can grip our lives when we see no way out of a situation. Stress can become intensified when people face an extreme situation in which there doesn't seem to be a solution—such as personal bankruptcy, abuse, a broken relationship, terminal illness, the death of a loved one, moral failure, national economic collapse, or a natural disaster.

People are left perplexed, not knowing what to do or where to go. Despair and discouragement flood their hearts because they feel that "everything is over" for them.

In such circumstances, individuals may be overcome by anger or depression and thus make destructive decisions, such as abandoning their family or committing suicide. Others live with a type of post-traumatic stress disorder, in which they feel anxious and full of fear, even after the danger or serious situation has passed. This condition disrupts their life and the lives of those around them.

Once again, let me assure you that, even in extreme situations, there is a way out of the damaging cycle of stress. In this book, I will demonstrate how Jesus Christ has the power to heal your emotional and spiritual wounds, strengthen your faith, and give you hope.

Jesus Christ opens a way where
there is no way.

CONSEQUENCES OF STRESS

Recurring or momentous stress clearly leads to negative consequences. The following is a summary of its destructive results.

Mental and Emotional Problems

A person who is under continuous stress becomes an easy target of mental, emotional, and physical problems. They may experience a loss of mental concentration, unremitting negative thoughts, feelings of despair, or lack of purpose. Some may begin to abuse drugs, alcohol, or other harmful substances. This can lead to a breakdown in normal, daily living.

Physical Issues

When people experience chronic stress, they may develop illnesses, such as arthritis, heart disease, or cancer. Additionally, while aging is a natural and inevitable process, premature aging is connected to stress, while longevity is connected to the absence of stress. "A wide range of studies have shown that the stress caused by things like: untreated depression, social isolation, long-term unemployment, anxiety attacks...can speed-up the aging process by shortening the length of each DNA strand."[7]

I have seen many men in executive positions age rapidly. I have even seen pastors and other Christian leaders who, being extremely busy in the work of the ministry, end up being attacked by stress. Although they are serving the Lord, they

7. Christopher Bergland, "Emotional Distress Can Speed Up Cellular Aging," *The Athlete's Way* blog, *Psychology Today*, April 7, 2014, https://www.psychologytoday.com/us/blog/the-athletes-way/201404/emotional-distress-can-speed-cellular-aging.

are often doing so in their own strength rather than His. One way to grow old quickly is to live under continual stress!

Stress creates conditions for the body to become more vulnerable to disease.

Breakdown of the Family

Perpetual stress within families can cause a breakdown of relationships and an absence of peace and order in the household. The family can become dysfunctional, bringing serious consequences such as hurtful arguments, jealousy, and divorce.

Poor Decision-Making

When you are making an important decision, stress is one of your worst advisers. A person who lives under a high state of stress can make poor decisions for the following reasons: (1) they feel rushed or tired and do not take time to think things through; (2) they are more susceptible to accepting incomplete or erroneous information; (3) they fall into a state of resignation, thinking they have limited solutions or options. Thus, their observations, determinations, and judgments are greatly lacking. Many people ask me how they can be sure they are making a good decision. I tell them the key is to feel the peace of

God in your spirit. Where there is stress, there is a lack of peace; under these conditions, it is difficult to make the best decisions.

Toxic Environments

A chronically stressed person can created a toxic environment for the people around them—at home, at work, in the community, and elsewhere—as they emanate anxiety, depression, bitterness, and other negative emotions. This can cause breakdowns in relationships, poor communication, decreased effectiveness, and, at times, unhealthy or unsafe conditions.

HOPE IN THE MIDST OF STRESS

If you have allowed anxiety, fear, overcommitment, lack of time, family issues, financial need, serious illness, or anything else to disrupt your peace and oppress your life, you need to be set free. I invite you to join me in the following prayer. Please pray aloud and with faith, knowing that Jesus is listening to you and cares about you.

Lord Jesus, I thank You for helping me understand what is happening in my life. I recognize that I have given place to fears and anxiety; I have let overcommitment, financial difficulty, health issues, or family problems become a cause of stress for me. I have tried unsuccessfully to control my situation or do more than I am able to—and the only results I have obtained are to lose my peace of mind, injure my health, and decrease my faith. I recognize that, instead of looking to You, I have tried to solve everything on my own, and I am exhausted! I feel anxious, irritable, and impatient. I feel there is no way out.

Today, I release my burdens to you, and I ask You to fill my heart with Your peace. I renounce stress, anxiety, spiritual oppression, and anything else the devil wants to bring into my life. I receive Your presence, Your grace, and Your power to liberate and strengthen me. I receive Your faith to believe that everything that is disordered in my life will become ordered again, and everything that is pending will end well. I rest in Your presence, placing my total trust and confidence in You. I give You control of my life. I worship You. Thank You, Jesus, for the complete provision You made on the cross of Calvary so that today, I can be free. Amen!

TRUE STORIES OF OVERCOMING OPPRESSIVE STRESS

Freed from Abandonment and Abuse

Tammy began to deal with depression from an early age. She had cycles of stress that led to anxiety attacks due to her father's absence and the verbal abuse she suffered. Things got worse until the Spirit of God delivered her:

Before I came to the Lord, my biggest struggle was with depression and anxiety. It all started because I grew up without my father, who would come and go between the United States and Venezuela, attending to business. At first, he was absent for days, then for weeks, and then for years. He would tell me he was coming, but then he did not come; his promises were false. This abandonment impacted my sense of identity and filled me with sadness.

Another family member began to verbally abuse me every day. He told me I was useless, that my family did not love me, and that I had been a mistake, an accident. People who saw what was happening advised me not to listen to him, explaining that he was like that. They didn't think his words would affect me because I was so young, but they did affect me—a lot.

For as long as I could remember, I had lived with depression because the enemy attacked me. During elementary school, I used to lock myself in the bathroom to cry, without knowing why. Although I was a very intelligent girl, the pressure to want to be the best was too much for me. I always believed I was expected to be the best in everything. I started thinking about suicide, but I did not know how to do it. I just wanted to sleep and never wake up; I did not want to keep dealing with this.

The first time I verbalized these thoughts, I was immediately admitted to a psychiatric unit. I was only twelve years old and they imposed the Baker Act on me. [8] I spent forty-eight hours there. The impact was such that my condition worsened. In that place, I saw what other children did to deal with these issues, and there I learned to cut my wrists. When I left the hospital, I began to see a therapist. They offered me medication, but I refused to take it. I knew I needed help, but I did not want it. I kept hearing voices in my head. I thought that medicine made me feel worse, but I couldn't say this to the therapist. After my experience in the hospital, I had lost trust in people. I did not want to say how I really felt because I was afraid to go back to that place.

In high school, my situation became worse because I had access to social networks and phones, and I was in an environment where popularity was all-important. At that time, I began to deal with anxiety and panic attacks. Since I was not very popular, I suffered alone. There were times when I would lock myself in but could not contain my negative thoughts. It was

8. The Baker Act is a law in the state of Florida (USA) that allows a person to call the authorities to provide emergency mental health services and temporary detention of one of their family members, even against their will, provided that this has been previously approved by a judge and is executed by mental health professionals.

as if someone was shouting in my mind with my own voice, reminding me of my mistakes and telling me that I would never achieve anything. This led me to hate my life.

It was very difficult for me to be happy and positive, and I started to suffer nervous breakdowns. This began to affect my social life because every time I went out with friends, they would have to carry me out of the car because fear had paralyzed me. I will never forget the first time this happened. It was after a high school party, and my mother's friends had to carry me out of the car because my whole body was shaking and I could not get out by myself.

I felt like I was in a cave on the other side of the world, screaming and crying out for help, being unable to walk, and feeling that nobody was listening to me. I smoked marijuana and cigarettes; I cut my body; I did whatever it took to relieve myself, but everything was in vain. My anxiety increased to dangerous levels. I couldn't sleep, so I started taking sleeping pills; but then I slept too many hours a day, and when I woke up, everything was worse.

The depression, anxiety, and stress that my experiences at school produced in me were very strong. The stress of social media, the stress of wanting to be a happy girl and doing the best for my family—everything burdened me, and I could not find a way out.

One day, I was invited to a House of Peace gathering connected with King Jesus Ministry. There, I experienced the presence of God, I received Jesus in my heart, and I was freed from all oppression. The depression, the anxiety, the stress, and the rejection related to my family and friends disappeared. Jesus set me free!

Amid the stress produced by anxiety, fear, and a lack of identity, Tammy received Jesus, and He transformed her life. Everything changed when she surrendered the control of her life to Christ. Whether instantaneous or over time, you too can experience the same if you accept Jesus in your heart and allow Him to heal you!

Healed of Blindness

Douglas is a Christian who lives in New Zealand and spent five years struggling with a degenerative disease in his eyes. This affected his life and his faith so much that he went from discouragement to frustration to despair. Stress robbed him of his trust in God, peace, and ministry, until he attended a conference sponsored by King Jesus Ministry.

Five years ago, I was operated on to remove a "fleshy" growth in my left eye, called a pterygium.

Apparently, it was a simple operation, but after the surgery, I noticed that something was wrong because my eye hurt a lot. I went back to the doctor and he told me that it was normal, but the pain did not go away. I went to another specialist who did several tests, and his diagnosis was acute aggressive glaucoma. This is a degenerative eye disease that usually affects older people and leads to blindness. But I was young, and the doctor worried about the rapid advance of the disease. They gave me medication to stop its progress, but every time I went for a medical checkup, I had less vision. All this happened in a matter of seven months.

I had always been a very active person. I owned a company, I liked boating, and I felt physically fit. Suddenly, this eye condition appeared, seemingly out of nowhere, and I felt as if my legs had been cut out from under me. I didn't know what to do! I was very afraid of going blind and not be able to do anything. I was a Christian and I had faith, but I had prayed, and nothing had happened.

As the glaucoma continued to progress, the doctor decided to do another surgery. After the procedure, I spent forty-eight hours with my left eye bandaged, in total darkness. I started to hear a voice in my head saying, "This is how you're going to live the rest of your life." I was horrified! Sadness flooded me. I thought that I would never see my wife again and never see my children or grandchildren grow. We went to whatever specialists we could find, but they all said the same thing. The disease was advancing at an accelerated pace!

One day, when I was leaving the office of a specialist, I saw a group of blind people with their canes; it was like watching my life walking in front of me. Despair began to grow inside me, until I got to the point of accepting that this would be my life. I used to lead a prayer ministry in my church and I had seen great miracles when praying for others, but I could not overcome this disease that seemed to have a life of its own and had surpassed my faith, so I left the ministry.

Later, someone told me that Apostle Guillermo Maldonado was going to hold a conference in my country. By that time, I was no longer interested in being healed. I only went to the conference because I was looking to reconnect with God and my faith. I had gone through so many things, so many people had prayed for me, and I had so many unfulfilled expectations that I was fed up. I was disillusioned about my faith, God, and everything. That was my state of mind when I went to the conference. However, I wanted to feel the Father's heart again.

With the first song, I could feel God's presence, and I think that was enough for me. The fear, the despair, the anger, and the frustration left. At that moment, the apostle asked everyone who needed prayer and healing to raise their hands. The man who was sitting next to me raised his hand, and then I did too. I began to pray for him first, for his family and his health; and then, the faith I used to have started coming back and I could feel the power of God. It was as if the life of God flowed through me. I finished praying and then asked the others to pray for me. I knew the state of my vision: because I was blind in my left eye, it was difficult for me to read my own writing or work on the computer, much less see road signs. But I just put my hands over my eyes and waited on God.

After I was prayed for, I did not feel anything special, yet when I picked up my notebook, I could read everything perfectly! I closed one eye and kept seeing perfectly. I closed the other eye and could still see perfectly. My healing was not due to medical science or anything I could have done for myself. I had tried everything—I had changed my diet and exercise routine, I had taken medications, I had taken vitamins—but nothing had helped. Today, I thank God because He saved and healed me!

Before God healed Douglas's sight, He restored the faith he had lost and freed his troubled and stressed spirit. Then Douglas could receive the healing he longed for. What Jesus did for Douglas, He can also do for you, right where you are, now! Ask God to set you free from your stress and bring healing to your life.

3

THE SECRET OF "RESTING"

Rest is a principle that is built into creation, and it is a great deterrent to stress. God created the heavens and the earth in six periods that He called days. After He made the world, the Bible tells us, *"And on the seventh day God ended His work which He had done, and He **rested** on the seventh day from all His work which He had done"* (Genesis 2:2). When it says that God *"rested,"* it does not mean that He was tired and had to spend time renewing His energy. Instead, it means that He ceased from working for a time after completing what He had set out to do.

Later, in the law that He gave to the Israelites through Moses, God instructed the people to rest one day a week:

"Remember the Sabbath day, to keep it holy. Six days you shall labor and do all your work, but the seventh day is the Sabbath of the LORD your God. In it you shall do no work" (Exodus 20:8–10). This was to be a day of rest for the people, and also for their animals. Everything that God created carries in its DNA the need for rest.

God also established other forms of rest for His people to follow. For example, after six consecutive years of planting and harvesting, they were to allow the land to lie uncultivated for a year: *"But in the seventh year there shall be a sabbath of solemn rest for the land, a sabbath to the LORD. You shall neither sow your field nor prune your vineyard"* (Leviticus 25:4). Various periods of "rest" were established not only for people to renew their strength, but also for them to stop and focus on their Creator and other important areas of their lives and to look out for the needs of others. (See Exodus 23:10–11.)

> *Everything that God created carries in its DNA the need for rest.*

Therefore, when the Scriptures speak of "rest," they are referring to something integral to our lives. Resting means putting aside all busy, strenuous activity—whether physical or mental—and regaining our strength and focus in the midst of stillness. It means having periods of respite not only physically and in our natural environment, but also in our spiritual being. Each type of rest is important for achieving true freedom from stress. It is useless to spend all day in bed if we are unable to physically sleep due to mental or emotional anguish. Neither will physical rest alone help us much if our spirit is oppressed by stress. What God wants for us is a rest that is whole and complete, one that covers all areas of our life.

RESTING IN GOD

The phrase "resting in God" means to give the Lord absolute control over our life and future. This shows God that we fully trust in Him and His purposes for us. When we put our burdens in His hands, we strip ourselves of all anxiety and worry. Only God knows the future, and He alone is in control. That's why we need to learn to surrender to Him and give Him our worries, just as Jesus taught us:

> *Therefore I say to you, do not worry about your life, what you will eat or what you will drink; nor about your body, what you will put on. Is not life more than food and the body more than clothing? Look at the birds of the air, for they neither sow nor reap nor gather into barns; yet your heavenly Father feeds them. Are you not of more value than they?... Therefore do not worry about tomorrow, for*

tomorrow will worry about its own things. Sufficient for the day is its own trouble. (Matthew 6:25–26, 34)

Stress is always connected to an area of our life that we have not yet surrendered to God. Often, we experience stress because of the struggle that exists between our flesh (our fallen human nature, which we continue to battle against in this life) and our spirit (our inner being, made alive in Christ). If we do not surrender a particular area to God, it becomes a heavy burden to us. Remember that when we become chronically stressed over something, we can emanate a "toxic" flow, creating a negative atmosphere that contaminates the people around us and leads them to feel sorry for us or distance themselves from us. In contrast, when we are full of faith and trust in God, then His anointing, grace, and favor will flow from us, attracting others to us and opening doors for us wherever we go.

> *Spiritual stress is the product of unnecessary worry.*

If we worry about the future to the point of becoming enslaved to stress, it is because we have not learned to trust God or His promises. Jesus tells us, *"In the world you will have tribulation; but be of good cheer, I have overcome the world*" (John 16:33). When we rest in God, we can have peace and joy in any circumstance, knowing that He is taking care of our needs as we continue to do our part—whatever comes under our human responsibilities. For example, we trust Him to free us from debt while we follow good financial practices. The greatest blessings come when we rest in God's love, goodness, and faithfulness.

The Bible speaks of God's rest when it says, "*Casting all your care upon Him, for He cares for you*" (1 Peter 5:7). What does it mean to "cast" our cares or anxieties upon God? It means to relinquish our worry, recognizing that we don't need to resolve matters in our own strength. We can place our absolute trust in Him to work on our behalf. For instance, the state of our business should no longer worry us, because we acknowledge that God is the ultimate Owner of that business and we are only His administrator. Or, conflict in our church should no longer cause us anxiety, because the church is not ours—it belongs to Christ. When we become stressed, we are telling God that we do not believe He can solve something that we have already tried to solve but could not. Therefore, if situations in our business, church, work, family, or health are causing us stress, we must immediately commit them to God.

We should know that as long as we hold on to our worries, the enemy will increase the pressure against us, bringing these concerns to our mind over and over again and creating an oppressive pattern of stress. When we enter into such a cycle, that is when stress becomes demonic. One of the evidences of demonic activity in a person is impatience, lack of rest, and lack of sleep. If the enemy manages to rob us of our peace—and with it, our sleep—stress becomes inevitable. Little by little, a lack of rest opens the way to demonic activity.

For this reason, the Bible encourages us, *"Do not present your members* [any part of your mind or body] *as instruments of unrighteousness to sin, but present yourselves to God as being alive from the dead, and your members as instruments of righteousness to God"* (Romans 6:13). As we give ourselves fully to God, cycles of stress can be broken.

Everything that we have not surrendered to God produces stress in our life.

THE PLACE OF SURRENDER

When Jesus was about to be falsely arrested and killed, He went to the garden of Gethsemane, one of His favorite places to rest and pray. There, He had to deal with the emotional, spiritual, and physical pressure that came from knowing that in just a few hours, He would die nailed to a cross.

> [Jesus] *knelt down and prayed, saying, "Father, if it is Your will, take this cup away from Me; nevertheless not My will, but Yours, be done." Then an angel appeared to Him from heaven, strengthening Him. And being in agony, He prayed more earnestly. Then His sweat became like great drops of blood falling down to the ground.*
> (Luke 22:41–44)

Gethsemane is a word of Chaldean origin that describes a large stone that was used to press olives in order to extract the oil. In this garden, Jesus was pressured to such an extent that it produced tremendous stress. How do we know? Because of the evidence offered by the Scriptures, where it says that *"His sweat became like great drops of blood falling down to the ground."* Undoubtedly, this stress was produced by knowing, in the Spirit, that He had to surrender His will and die a dreadful death to fulfill the will of the Father.

The great exchange of the cross was about to occur; Jesus, the sinless Son of God, would die in our place. In this way, humanity, a race of sinners, could be forgiven of their sin and reconciled with the heavenly Father. Jesus's life was not taken away from Him by anyone. Because of His deep love for us, He voluntarily laid it down Himself to fulfill the will of the Father. (See John 10:17–18.) Thus, He was able to see ahead to the eternal fruit of His surrender and enter into the Father's rest. *"Looking unto Jesus, the author and finisher of our faith, who for the joy that was set before Him endured the cross, despising the shame, and has sat down at the right hand of the throne of God"* (Hebrews 12:2).

Fully surrendering our will to God is the key to living without stress.

The kind of stress Jesus experienced at Gethsemane would easily have led any other person to succumb to the temptation of renouncing their purpose in order to preserve their physical life. But not Jesus. He was both fully God and fully man. As a man, I'm sure He would have preferred not to go to Calvary and die; that is why He had to pray intensely before yielding to His purpose on earth and fulfilling the will of the Father. Relatively speaking, we experience a similar process. When we face taking an action that our will greatly opposes, or something that causes us tremendous anxiety or fear—or when we have acted in a way that is contrary to what God would want—we can experience suffocating stress. Jesus understands what we are going through. That is why He said, *"Come to Me, all you who labor and are heavy laden, and I will give you rest. Take My yoke upon you and learn from Me, for I am gentle and lowly in heart, and you will find rest for your souls. For My yoke is easy and My burden is light"* (Matthew 11:28–30).

In this passage, Jesus teaches us that when we follow a path that is the opposite of God's will, we carry a very heavy burden. Among the heavy burdens people can take on are sexual immorality, oppressive relationships, jealousy, addictions, and depression. When we carry such a burden, our movements in the natural, just as much as in the spiritual, conform to that burden. Even our thought patterns adapt to the burden we carry and prevent us from seeing a way out. But today, Jesus tells us, "Give Me the burden that the world has placed on you or you have taken on yourself—the burden that oppresses and enslaves you—and in return, I will give you My 'yoke,' which is easy, and My 'burden,' which is light." Following God's guidance and purpose for our lives brings us relief. When we give God all our burdens, we can live stress-free.

The yoke of the world is a very heavy burden that does not let us rest.

HOW TO ENTER INTO GOD'S REST

The times we live in are often chaotic, and there is turmoil all around us. I believe we are in a period called the "end times," when the world as we know it will soon be coming to a conclusion, culminating with the return of Jesus Christ and the defeat of the devil and all those who oppose God. However, even in the midst of confusion, disagreements, divisions, and spiritual warfare (the enemy's attacks against us), we can enter into our heavenly Father's rest and remain in that rest. God gave us one of the keys to stress-free living when He said, *"Be still, and know that I am God"* (Psalm 46:10).

Receive Jesus as Your Savior

It is necessary for us to know and apply the revelation that leads us to rest in God so that we can receive His promises. The first step, if you have not already done so, is to accept Jesus Christ as your Savior, believing that He died on the cross in your place so your sins can be forgiven and you can receive new life in Him and begin to follow His ways. Jesus calls all who have accepted Him "the church." (See Matthew 16:18.) This does not refer to membership in a particular church or denomination, but to being a redeemed child of God and a citizen of His kingdom. In this end-time cycle, God continues to guide His church to rest in Him. Peter, one of Jesus's closest disciples, wrote the following: *"Therefore humble yourselves under the mighty hand of God, that He may exalt you in due time, casting all your care upon Him, for He cares for you"* (1 Peter 5:6–7).

The Father has promised that before Christ's return, His church will enter into His rest.

Receive God's "Times of Refreshing"

The second step is to receive God's *"times of refreshing."* The apostle Peter said,

> *Repent therefore and be converted, that your sins may be blotted out, so that times of refreshing may come from the presence of the Lord, and that He may send Jesus Christ, who was preached to you before, whom heaven must receive until the times of restoration of all things, which God has spoken by the mouth of all His holy prophets since the world began.* (Acts 3:19–21)

The Bible gives us various principles—both physical and spiritual—that lead us to enjoy times of refreshing. Among these principles are the following: putting all work on pause during the day of rest, or Sabbath (see, for example, Exodus 23:12); making sure we keep hydrated after a physical activity (see, for example, Judges 15:18–19); listening to uplifting music (see, for example, 1 Samuel 16:23); and having fellowship with other believers in Jesus who can strengthen us (see, for example, 2 Timothy 1:16).

God has promised that the church can enjoy rest in the midst of turmoil, experiencing these times of refreshing, by uniting our hearts with His in deep intimacy and trust. In contrast, those who do not enter God's rest will end up stressed and exhausted. The rest God provides goes beyond any natural provision—it is *super*natural, since it comes from the heavenly realm through His Spirit.

As we read in Acts 3:19, we experience times of refreshing or rest by remaining in the *"presence of the Lord,"* because it is in His presence where we find all we need. In Psalm 23, David describes the Lord as a good Shepherd who provides everything necessary for His sheep so they will not have anything to worry about: *"The LORD is my shepherd; I shall not want"* (Psalm 23:1). The book of Psalms also reveals that, in addition to rest, being in God's presence gives us joy: *"You will show me the path of life; in Your presence is fullness of joy; at Your right hand are pleasures forevermore"* (Psalm 16:11).

> *What separates the church from the world is supernatural rest.*

What is the primary obstacle that prevents us from finding and entering into God's rest? It is sin, or rebellion against Him and His ways. It was the emergence of sin in the world that first brought confusion, disorder, pain, suffering, envy, lies, sickness, and death to the human race. (See, for example, Romans 5:12; James 4:1–4.) Moreover, most people who are living in sin—especially after having become believers in Christ—are constantly fleeing and hiding from the presence of God. Their souls find no peace or quiet; they are unable to rest mentally, emotionally, or spiritually. (See, for example, Genesis 4:13–14.) Therefore, if you are in sin and want to return to the presence of God, you must repent and follow Him in obedience once more. Turn away from your sin, ask God to forgive you, and accept His complete forgiveness so you can again receive *"times of refreshing…from the presence of the Lord."*

Only repentance restores our ability to rest in God's presence.

SIGNS OF RESTING IN GOD

There are three unmistakable signs that we have entered into the rest of God:

1. We Have Peace

It is impossible to be in the presence of God and not have peace. The Bible promises us:

> *Be anxious for nothing, but in everything by prayer and supplication, with thanksgiving, let your requests be made known to God; and the peace of God, which surpasses all understanding, will guard your hearts and minds through Christ Jesus.*   (Philippians 4:6–7)

When we repent of our sins and receive God's forgiveness, He fills us with His peace. When we give God our burdens, He lifts them from us and gives us His peace. When we surrender our will to Him, He fulfills His will in our lives and immerses us in His peace. Again, this is not a natural peace but a supernatural one. The peace we receive is not just a peace in which there is an absence of conflict. Instead, it is a peace that elevates us above any conflict and leads us to transcend the natural and live in the supernatural. Thus, having God's peace is one of the unmistakable signs that we have entered into His rest.

2. We Worship God

Heartfelt worship arises from being in a place of intimacy with God. When we are living in God's rest, we do not worship Him only when things are going well and we have no problems. Rather, even in the midst of the harshest storm or the darkest night of our life, we choose to give Him the place of preeminence and worship Him in that place of rest. Only when we surrender to God can we worship Him, as Jesus expressed, "*in spirit and truth*" (John 4:23, 24).

If we are stressed, we cannot worship God in this way. However, there are times when we may start to worship Him in the flesh, doing it in our own strength with our mind, body, or emotions, because stress is controlling us. However, seeing our genuine desire to worship Him, God will then send His Holy Spirit to come and help us to worship Him in spirit and truth. When this happens, our stress fades away as we enter into the rest of God's presence.

3. We Continuously Allow God to Be in Control

When we are stressed, we cannot see, hear, or discern what is happening in the spiritual world; our spiritual senses are blocked, and we only perceive what is occurring in the natural realm. However, when we enter into the rest of the Lord, we live in continual anticipation of seeing the next thing that God will do. We do not conform to the impossibilities declared by natural minds, but we faithfully expect the Lord to act in supernatural power. The greatest miracle we can experience is to see God do what is impossible for us.

You will not see how God is acting in your favor until you commit to resting in Him, releasing your worries to His care.

This is not something that is achieved overnight; it takes time and persistence to change the way we handle problems and to understand the full meaning of "resting." In one sense, resting in God's presence makes us spectators of what He is doing. However, this doesn't mean that we are to be indifferent as we wait for His intervention, because He desires that we participate in His purposes. Rather, it means learning to daily live by faith, always expecting the "something new" that He will do. We will learn more about the exercise of our faith in the next chapter.

> *When we rest in God, our stress is released, because to rest in God is to live in total faith.*

REMOVING THE BURDENS

Do you want receive a movement of God's Holy Spirit in your life so you can stop living in a state of continual stress? Do you want to experience a time of refreshing in your family, your relationships, your business, your ministry, or your plans for the future? Enter into the presence of God and rest in Him. In His presence, He will deal with your heart, because true change begins in the heart. There are areas and circumstances in your life that God will change only when you remain "still," acknowledging that He is in control of your life and allowing Him to do what you are unable to do.

To be set free, we must remove the burdens that keep us enslaved and lead us to live under stress. Removing these burdens is not difficult if we do so in the power of Jesus. *"It shall come to pass in that day that his burden will be taken away from your shoulder, and his yoke from your neck, and the yoke will be destroyed because of the anointing oil"* (Isaiah 10:27). Jesus Himself did not do anything without the approval of the Father because He lived in total dependence on Him. (See John 5:19, 30; 8:28.) It is not God's plan for us to live under continual stress. Let us follow Jesus's example and live in the peace our heavenly Father desires for us.

I want to pray for you now because I know that God will work a miracle in your situation as you follow the principles I have outlined in this chapter, committing yourself to surrender to and trust Him in order to live a life free of stress. Then, you will see the glory of God in the midst of every adverse circumstance you go through while you remain in His presence and experience His peace and joy.

Beloved Father, I come before You, presenting to You every person who is reading this book. Thank You for guiding me to write *Stress-Free Living* and for giving me Your revelation and power to undo the works of the devil.

I ask You to send Your Holy Spirit to each reader. In Your name, I release upon them deliverance, healing, and superabundant peace. In the name of Jesus, I cast out every spirit of anxiety, depression, and stress that is oppressing their lives. I declare that they enter into Your presence and that Your peace floods their hearts. I declare that they find rest in Your presence, by Your grace and by the finished work of Christ on the cross. I declare that Your presence destroys all affliction and lack of faith. I declare that, right now, they are full of Your faith to live in complete certainty that You will deal with each of their impossibilities. I release Your supernatural power to perform miracles in their health, their finances, and their personal, work, and ministry relationships. I declare Your presence over their lives.

I give You thanks, Lord, because I know that great miracles are already happening in the lives of Your children. I give all the glory, honor, and praise to You forever. Amen!

TRUE STORIES OF OVERCOMING OPPRESSIVE STRESS

Freed from Financial Stress

The Arias family from San Antonio, Texas, USA, shared a wonderful testimony about how the financial stress that had come upon their household disappeared when they decided to rest in God.

Seeing God's power at work in King Jesus Ministry urged us to take our relationship with Him to a new dimension. Some time ago, a very strong hurricane hit San Antonio, and our house suffered serious damage. It was a heavy blow to my husband and me and our five children; we were wondering how we were going to resolve this. The situation had become very difficult. We were under great stress. We had been believing God for a new house for a long time, so we wanted to sell our home; but then, a new storm came, this time with hail, which caused a lot of damage to the roof. The stress increased because months passed, and we did not receive the insurance money to make repairs to the roof and windows. Everything was broken, and we had to live in the house like this. Our dream of a new house was delayed and the pressure increased.

One day, the contractor came and gave us a quote, but he did not come back to do the work. Then, we decided to trust God and become partners with King Jesus Ministry because we understood that when we help to advance the kingdom of God, a great blessing comes. So, we took a step of faith and sowed our first seed during an event that we attended as part of our spiritual training. On the day we returned home after the event, we called the contractor who had previously ignored us and asked him to do the roof work. He replied, "I'll be at your home in fifteen minutes." We had never before heard him say anything like that!

However, we still had not received the insurance money. In faith, we decided to call the real estate agent and resume our search for a new house. We filled out the paperwork and promised the agent that the roof of our current home would be fixed when the time came to sell our house. Two weeks later, we found the house of our dreams. We made an offer, but then we had a new setback: my husband's credit score was good, but mine wasn't. I needed my credit to go up fifty points supernaturally. One day, the person responsible for preapproving the loan said, "I don't know why I'm doing this, but we are going to make the offer in faith, trusting that in two weeks your credit will go up." Nobody does that! We submitted our offer, along with four other potential buyers, for a house located in an area that everyone in San Antonio wants to live in because the houses are beautiful and gain value quickly. Our offer was the lowest, but, by the grace of God, my credit score went up, and the owners chose us. The real estate agent called to give us the good news; but, in the middle of the great celebration, we realized that our house was still in the midst of being repaired, and we had to sell it.

The pressure was strong, but again, we decided to believe God. We put our house up for sale—once more, with the promise that all the repairs would be finished before the sale was completed. My husband called the insurance company and demanded that they send the money because it had been a year since the storm had destroyed our roof and windows. The insurance company replied that they did not understand what had happened, but the check was already in the mail.

What had been delayed for a year was solved in a few days as soon as we rested in God and made a covenant with Him. Everything was accelerated! This was a great testimony for our children because we lived the whole process together. They witnessed the fact that in the midst of a great problem, we could rest in God; and when we made a covenant with Him to advance His kingdom, everything that had been stopped accelerated in a supernatural way. God continues to work miracles!

This family could easily have fallen into despair in the middle of a very complicated situation. They could have been depressed, accepting the idea that everything was lost and they would have to wait years to even think about buying a house. However, they decided to believe the God of the impossible. They made a decision to give Him control over everything, and God responded with one miracle after another. The same can happen to you!

Healed of a Severe Physical Condition

A thirty-four-year-old woman named Hui-Han Huang attended one of King Jesus Ministry's Supernatural Encounter meetings in Taiwan. She was unable to walk, but the power of God healed her, and she was freed from anguish and despair.

Three years ago, I took a Chinese medicine that is made from herbs, which had been bought on the black market. Apparently, it contained a very strong poison. Because of this, my immune system collapsed. My heart and nervous system were severely affected; both my legs became inflamed, and the pain was so intense that I could not walk or even stand up. This situation caused me deep anguish and despair. The worst thing was that the doctors could not find a solution, and this led me to experience great stress. The day they ministered healing at the Supernatural Encounter conference, the fire and power of God impacted me in such a way that my body began to tremble. I felt God's power! Last night, I did not have the strength to stand up. Now, I can walk. I was even able to go up and down stairs. The power of God is real! Thank You, Jesus!

4

THREE PILLARS OF FAITH FOR OVERCOMING STRESS

*A*fter [Jesus] *had offered one sacrifice for sins forever,* [He] *sat down at the right hand of God, from that time waiting till His enemies are made His footstool"* (Hebrews 10:12–13). As we see in this portion of Scripture, after Jesus overcame death, being resurrected by the power of the Holy Spirit, He was received into heaven, and He sat down at the right hand of the Father. The fact that He is seated at the Father's right hand doesn't mean He isn't still active and working in our lives. He continually intercedes for us and moves on our behalf. (See Romans 8:34.) However, He rests in the sense that His victory on the cross over sin, the devil, and sickness is *complete* and *final.*

One of the tactics of the enemy is to cause us to wear ourselves down through our own efforts. As Christians who have put our faith and trust in Jesus Christ, we need to rest in God before, during, and after each spiritual battle we wage in His power. However, if our faith is lacking, or we do not understand how God is working, we may try to fight against the enemy in our own strength, even if this leads us into stressful situations. A Christian who recognizes that God is stronger than the adversary stands aside and observes how the Almighty fights on their behalf and gives them the victory.

Many people in the church, which is also called *"the body of Christ"* (1 Corinthians 12:27), are still immersed in an endless struggle against the enemy. They have not understood that once they give a burden to God, they must let Him act sovereignly and defend them. Simply put, they must allow God to be God.

Jesus's life demonstrates one of the greatest expressions of faith we can manifest: no matter what is happening to us or around us, nothing and no one can cause us anxiety, and we are continually able to rest in God. For example, one time, after Jesus had preached to a multitude and healed their diseases, He and His disciples got into a boat and began to cross the Sea of Galilee. On the way, a great storm broke out, and they were about to be shipwrecked. During the commotion of the storm, Jesus was sleeping peacefully in the stern. The disciples were full of fear, so they woke Jesus up. He stood and firmly rebuked the winds and the sea, and the storm immediately ceased. Then He admonished His disciples, telling them, *"Why are you fearful, O you of little faith?"* (Matthew 8:26).

When we face problems, most of us would like to rest in the way Jesus did on that boat, without anything disturbing us. We would also like to be able to overcome our storms in the power of God. And this is possible! However, it requires revelation of three fundamental pillars that sustain our faith so that we are able to live free of stress: (1) applying the finished work of the cross; (2) resting in God's presence; and (3) receiving the supernatural grace of God.

One of the greatest expressions of faith we can manifest is when nothing worries us and we can rest in God.

THREE PILLARS THAT SUSTAIN OUR FAITH
Applying the Finished Work of the Cross

As I described earlier, Jesus went to the cross voluntarily. There, He gave His life because He knew that His main purpose on earth was to rescue humanity from the bondage of the devil and lead us back to the Father. He died on the cross to pay for all the sins, diseases, and misery of the human race.

"But He was wounded for our transgressions, He was bruised for our iniquities; the chastisement for our peace was upon Him, and by His stripes we are healed" (Isaiah 53:5). He paid the ransom price to free us from all physical, emotional, mental, and spiritual ailments; He delivered us from anxiety, fear, depression, and every other yoke of the enemy. Just before Jesus died, He said, *"It is finished!"* (John 19:30). That means, "It is completely paid." Rest comes to us when we understand and have total confidence in the finished work of the cross.

> *When we rest in the finished work of Christ on the cross, we have placed our faith and trust in Him.*

Once you believe in what God has said and done on your behalf, you can rest knowing that He is faithful to keep His promises. (See, for example, Hebrews 11:11.) You can have absolute confidence that, as you trust in the finished work of the cross, God will act in your best interests. However, we must remember that spiritual "resting" does not mean abandoning our work for God or failing to fulfill our human responsibilities. Resting in God means that we do everything that is possible, while He does the impossible! Rest leads us to wait with expectation for God to act and triumph over our difficulties. When we rest in Him, He gives us unusual grace and favor, opens doors for us that were formerly inaccessible, and guides us to receive what He desires to give us.

God has not called us to live in a state of stress, so we should not allow stress to control our life. Everything we need—now and in the future—was provided for us on the cross two thousand years ago. By faith, we can receive salvation, healing, miracles, transformation, provision, deliverance, and much more. Jesus paid for everything completely.

Stress comes when we try to do something that is not our responsibility or that only God can do.

However, the enemy is cunning and knows when we are resting in faith and when we are allowing ourselves to be stressed. If he sees you resting in an atmosphere of intimacy in the presence of God, then, for him, it is like reliving his absolute defeat by Jesus at Calvary. So today, begin to increase your faith. Speak to your circumstances—your financial problems, your marital conflict, your sickness, your depression, your children's rebellion, or anything else that is tormenting you—and say, "Jesus paid for this on the cross. Right now, I rest in His finished work and God's promises. I'm not going to become stressful. Jesus has already given me the victory; He has paid for the debt of sin I owed, and He has completely defeated the enemy."

> *True faith means resting in the finished*
> *work of Jesus on the cross,*
> *where everything has already been*
> *provided for us.*

Resting in God's Presence

The second pillar that sustains our faith is to rest in God's presence. In the previous chapter, we talked how we can eliminate our burdens by entering into the presence of God. We must learn to remain in His presence—the pure, unpolluted atmosphere that our heavenly Father designed human beings to live in at the time of their creation. In Genesis, this atmosphere is called "the garden of Eden." In my book *The Glory of God*, I explain that when human beings sinned, "Mankind did not fall from a place; it fell from God's presence, from the environment of glory."[9]

Eden was designed as a place of ongoing spiritual, emotional, mental, and physical rest. Although Adam and Eve

9. Guillermo Maldonado, *The Glory of God: Experience a Supernatural Encounter with His Presence* (New Kensington, PA: Whitaker House, 2012), 15.

worked by tending the garden, they experienced no interpersonal conflict, toil, or stress until they rebelled against God. When they disobeyed Him, they were removed from His presence, and humanity was not restored to that presence in a complete sense until Christ came to earth and reconciled us to the Father. The Bible tells us that after Jesus's death, the veil of the temple was torn from top to bottom (see Matthew 27:51; Luke 23:45), symbolizing that Jesus had opened up full access to the Father. From the time that Jesus restored us, believers have been able to enter confidently into God's presence. That is why Jesus told us, *"Come to Me, all you who labor and are heavy laden, and I will give you rest"* (Matthew 11:28).

When we are in the presence of the Lord, nothing that might happen around us or in the world can cause us to enter into a cycle of worry or fear, because we know that God is in control, as these Scriptures emphasize: *"For he who has entered His rest has himself also ceased from his works as God did from His"* (Hebrews 4:10). *"[God] said, 'My Presence will go with you, and I will give you rest'"* (Exodus 33:14).

> *Only in the presence of God will you find rest, peace, and joy to the fullest.*

In the presence of God, what we have previously struggled to accomplish can happen easily and in a short time due to the working of His supernatural power. I have frequently witnessed this truth firsthand in my life. There have been times when I have become worried and stressed due to the many burdens and responsibilities I carry, not only locally but also globally. Yet whenever I enter God's presence, everything changes. When I finish praying, worshipping, and communing with God, I feel rested. Why does this happen? First, because daily, in His presence, I recognize anew that God is my Father, I am His son, and He loves me. With these assurances, I simply give Him all my burdens. They are no longer under my control; I leave them in His hands. That is why I agree with the author of Hebrews, who encourages us, *"Let us therefore be diligent to enter that rest, lest anyone fall according to the same example of disobedience"* (Hebrews 4:11).

One of the reasons the devil tries to prevent us from entering into prayer and communion with God is that, in the presence of the Lord, there is no spiritual warfare. Because the enemy does not have access to God's presence, he cannot attack us there. Thus, he tries to distract us and wear us down so that, like him, we will not be able to drink from our Source of life. When we are removed from our Source, we end up dry and burned out. Let us always remember the answer to such a condition: *"**Repent** therefore and be converted, that your sins may be blotted out, so that times of refreshing may come from the* *presence of the Lord"* (Acts 3:19). Repentance is not something we do only once, at the beginning of our life in Christ; on the contrary, we must repent daily of any disobedience or lack of faith. Without true repentance, we cannot access the *"times of refreshing."*

How long should it take us to enter God's presence? If one is experienced in prayer and worship, it should not take much time, perhaps a few minutes. I have come to the place where it takes me seconds. In general, I can say that I live continually in God's presence, because I understand that this is the place for which I was designed. We were not created to enter His presence and then leave it, but to remain in it; therefore, staying in His presence should be our goal. Each time we seek God, we should be able to enter His presence faster and find it easier to do.

If you are facing situations that cause you stress, you urgently need to enter God's presence. When you go to your Source, He will remove every burden, give you rest, and work a miracle because in His presence, there is total provision.

There are people who do not receive the miracle they expect because they think that entering God's presence takes a long time, or that it is reserved only for pastors or very special believers. However, it is not like that. The sacrifice of Jesus opened the way so that all who believe in Him and confess

Him as Lord and Savior of their lives can enter into His presence.

> *God's revelation is not received by entering and leaving His presence but by living permanently in it.*

I am often asked the question, "How can we know that we are in the presence of God?" The first thing we find there is peace. We also feel a reverent fear and a sense of security and protection. Additionally, we are surrounded by His eternal, unconditional, supernatural love. Another unmistakable sign that we are in His presence is that we no longer feel the need to fight for what we need. Therefore, if you still feel burdened, if you are still striving against the enemy, you urgently need to enter into God's presence.

Receiving the Supernatural Grace of God

The third pillar that sustains our faith is to receive God's supernatural grace. "Grace" refers to being granted a favor, talent, or gift from God that we do not deserve. It includes the bestowal of His supernatural power, which enables us to be and do what we cannot achieve in our human capacity. In other words, grace is the ability God gives us to walk in the supernatural.

It is important to understand what God's grace really is because various doctrines about grace are preached today, some with very little biblical foundation. There are those who preach a false idea of grace that claims we have no responsibilities in our Christian life because Christ already did everything for us. This is a half-truth. It is true that the work of the cross is complete, but it is also true that we are to actively participate in God's purposes. *"For we are His workmanship, created in Christ Jesus for good works, which God prepared beforehand that we should walk in them"* (Ephesians 2:10).

Moreover, the enemy still roams the world doing evil. The Bible says that he *"walks about like a roaring lion, seeking whom he may devour"* (1 Peter 5:8). We are called to enforce Christ's victory on earth and make it remain in force day by day. We are to declare that Christ has triumphed and pray for His will to be done on earth as it is in heaven as we rest in God's presence. The most notable difference between spiritual warfare and natural warfare is that, by the grace of God, with spiritual warfare, victory is guaranteed.

In the New Testament, we see that the grace of God in Christ has a fundamental purpose: to pay for all the sins of mankind. It is through Jesus that those who have been rebellious against the Creator can experience grace—God's unmerited favor—and forgiveness, enabling them to walk in a relationship of intimacy with Him. Thus, the life, passion, death, and resurrection of Jesus come to us as evidence of the grace of God, acting to save mankind.

I must point out here that although God loves sinners, He does not tolerate sin. Therefore, according to divine justice, whoever does not recognize the work of Jesus on the cross is condemned, and the penalty is death. (See, for example, John 3:18; Romans 6:23.) People may try to cover up their evil and iniquity by doing works that outwardly look good. However, these works are unacceptable to God (see Ephesians 2:8–9) and only distract them from finding righteousness in Jesus, who is *"the way, the truth, and the life"* (John 14:6).

If you have been trying to cover up your sin, please confess it to God and receive the grace of His forgiveness. There is no sin so great that the blood of Christ cannot erase it. That is why the Scriptures state that *"where sin abounded, grace abounded much more"* (Romans 5:20). By God's grace, we have access to the Most Holy Place (God's presence) and to the provision of everything we may need in this life, now and in the future.

According to the Scriptures, God has released His grace in Christ Jesus to accomplish all these purposes:

+ To save us. *"For by grace you have been saved through faith, and that not of yourselves; it is the gift of God"* (Ephesians 2:8).

+ To conquer the enemy. *"And the God of peace will crush Satan under your feet shortly. The grace of our Lord Jesus Christ be with you"* (Romans 16:20).

+ To empower us to overcome sin in our lives. *"For sin shall not have dominion over you, for you are not under law but under grace"* (Romans 6:14).

+ To enable us to live in holiness. *"So now, brethren, I commend you to God and to the word of His grace, which is able to build you up and give you an inheritance among all those who are sanctified"* (Acts 20:32).

+ To empower us to live in true righteousness. *"I do not set aside the grace of God; for if righteousness comes through the law, then Christ died in vain"* (Galatians 2:21).

+ To enable us to fulfill our purpose and calling. *"[God] has saved us and called us with a holy calling, not according to our works, but according to His own purpose and grace which was given to us in Christ Jesus before time began"* (2 Timothy 1:9).

It would be impossible for us to be and do all these things without the supernatural grace of God. Again, we must understand that living in God's grace doesn't mean we aren't to give anything back to Him. On the contrary, we are to serve Him and His purposes with love, devotion, and faithfulness—all by His grace. In this regard, the apostle Paul writes, *"But by* the grace of God I am what I am, and His grace toward me was not in vain; but I labored more abundantly than they all, yet not I, but the grace of God which was with me" (1 Corinthians 15:10).

At first glance, it might seem contradictory for Paul to say that he became an apostle by the grace of God, and then add that he works more than the other apostles. Does this mean that he worked to earn God's favor? No! The works of the kingdom are accomplished from a place of grace. Paul worked hard, not to earn grace from God, but by taking hold of the grace he had been given in order to do the will of the Father. The only way to serve God free of stress is to do so as He planned for us—in the strength of His grace.

> *When we serve God, He gives us His supernatural grace, and we find rest in the midst of our hard work.*

I urge you to stop trying to work for God in your own strength. Understand that everything He commands us to do is impossible to accomplish with human strength; we can achieve it only by His grace. If you believe this, then from now on, seek to continually rest in God, and your life will begin to flow better. By the grace of God, we can be saved and made healthy, free, and prosperous; we can overcome the temptations of the enemy, do the work of the ministry, and fulfill the will of God. If you work in this way, you will not become exhausted, because you will depend on divine grace, not on your limited strength. As long as you try to work according to your own power, you will feel burdened and tired. But if you hold on to God's supernatural grace, He will renew your strength, and you will live in an atmosphere of rest.

Those who walk in the grace of God specialize in doing difficult things more easily.

ESTABLISHING THE PILLARS

Is your life supported by the three pillars—applying the finished work of the cross, resting in God's presence, and receiving His supernatural grace—that can sustain your faith and enable you to live free of stress? I invite you to pray with me and make a commitment to raising these pillars in your life:

Heavenly Father, I thank You for Your love and provision. I recognize that there are circumstances in my life that I have not surrendered to You, and they have now become out of control. I acknowledge that I have allowed stress, anxiety, and depression to gain a foothold, and I do not know how to get myself out of these conditions. I am sorry, Father, for not trusting You, for trying to solve my problems in my own strength without asking for Your help.

Forgive my lack of faith in not depending on You. Forgive me for not approaching Your presence with a contrite and humble heart. Today, I commit myself to surrender to You, and I place in Your hands all the pain, anxiety, depression, anguish, frustration, and depression that has flooded my heart. I need Your grace and the ministry of Your Holy Spirit to enter Your presence and find rest and help. I let go of my burdens and simply worship You; I ask that Your presence would fill my troubled mind and allow my spirit to become one with You again. I receive Your peace, love, faith, grace, and power.

I know that everything that has been going wrong in my life is now under Your control, and I will see Your hand of power working in my favor. I rest in Your presence, in the finished work of Christ on the cross, and in the grace that He released, so that today I can live in victory. I declare myself empowered to live by faith, as Christ did. As He overcame, I will overcome. I declare Your presence and power over my life. In the name of Jesus, amen!

TRUE STORIES OF OVERCOMING OPPRESSIVE STRESS

Shown a Way Out

Kelly lives in Miami, Florida. Before she came to King Jesus Ministry, she suffered from stress, depression, bipolar disorder, and suicidal thoughts, but the Lord rescued her!

I was still in high school the first time I tried to take my own life due to stress. It was an idea that constantly came to me! The doctors diagnosed me with bipolar disorder. I lived with anxiety. I did not know what to do, and I thought I was never going to come out of it. I spent seven years in this condition—fighting depression, stress, and the desire to commit suicide.

When I visited King Jesus Ministry, I felt the presence of God, and I felt rested. It was the first time I felt peace inside me. The stress went away, and I was free of the thoughts of death that had haunted my mind. The best thing that happened is that they taught me to use spiritual weapons to keep myself free. Something that happens with depression is that it makes you feel like there is no way out. But when they teach you to pray, to be free, and to keep your deliverance, when they tell you how the grace of God works and what our rights are as His children, then everything changes.

When we are equipped, the enemy loses control over our lives.

Today, I am free, and I know how to remain free! I know what to do so that the spirit of suicide never enters my life again, so that stress does not rob me of my peace or lead me to depression. Now, I know that there is a way out and that the grace of God is more than enough to give me peace, health, and hope. Glory to God!

What happened to Kelly can happen to you. God can exchange our anxiety for unparalleled rest. What do we need? To appropriate the work of Christ on the cross, remain in God's presence, and live according to His grace.

Given a New Identity and Life in Christ

Terry dealt with rejection and a lack of identity most of her life. At a young age, she was diagnosed with ADHD, depression, and other issues. These issues led her to consume alcohol and drugs. After she grew up, married, and had children, her entire family eventually left her, and she realized that her last hope was to seek God. The Lord used Terry's neighbor to guide her to freedom.

When I was four-and-a-half years old, I was given up for adoption because I suffered physical abuse from my biological parents. I began to present some abnormalities, such as fits of anger. The psychiatrist diagnosed me with mild mental retardation, but they could not do anything for me because I was very young. At age eleven, I was diagnosed with depression, anxiety, insomnia, and ADHD. My medicines were often changed and the doses were increased, but nothing worked.

I grew up going to a church, but I had no revelation of who God was. When I was thirteen, I began to consume alcohol, and at sixteen, I started smoking cigarettes and using drugs. Throughout my life, I always had some kind of drug in my system, but in 2014, I hit rock bottom. By that time, I had gotten married and had two children. On Father's Day, my husband told me that he was tired of the life he had with me and wanted to live alone. When he left, my son also left, but my daughter decided to stay with me. She spent three months living with me, but at that time, I started sinking further into drugs. One day, my daughter said to me, "Mom, I do not want to live with you anymore," and she left to live with her dad. That was the end for me. I remember shouting, "Enough! I do not want to live anymore." But afterward, I reconsidered. I knew that something had to change. I could not keep running away from reality!

Then, I remembered my neighbor. She was different. She was a Christian, and she had been inviting me to church for two years, but I always said no. When my daughter left, I felt I had lost everything. In search of a change, I went to my neighbor's House of Peace meeting. She received me with a few words that touched my heart. I felt the love of God in her. Later, I went to a conference at King Jesus Ministry, and there God healed my knee, which I had not been able to bend due to arthritis. I felt a fire in my knee, and suddenly, I could move it. That gave me faith to believe that I would not need any more antidepressants or pills to control the ADHD, insomnia, and anxiety. That day, I knew that God was real and continued to work miracles. That was the faith I needed!

When I went home after the conference, I threw all the drugs I had in the trash. Since that day, I have not taken them again. I do not need them! God also restored my marriage and my family, and everyone returned home to me. Previously, I could not sleep because of depression, but now I sleep in peace. I did not have a job, but now we have a business and will soon open another. Before, I used to say I hated God and blamed Him for everything. Now, I am so grateful to Him because He is good. I know He loves me, and His love is unconditional. I had always dreamed of having a life like this, but I thought it was impossible for me. Now, I know that I am a daughter of God. He has given me my life back. Christ has given me identity!

5

TIPS FOR STRESS-FREE LIVING

There is a solution for stress! When we are stressed, we often do not know what to do, and everything becomes chaotic. After God sets us free through His Holy Spirit, we must learn to stay in His rest and peace and not fall back into a stressful lifestyle. As we surrender to the Lord and let Him work in our lives, there is no type of stress that can control us, and any adverse situation can be resolved with His supernatural power. His grace will be our strength, we will receive His wisdom, and everything will work together for good if we remain in His love. (See Romans 8:28.)

In this final chapter, I want to give you a series of practical and spiritual tips to help you live stress-free as you continue to have faith in the finished work of Jesus on the cross, remain in God's presence, and live by His grace.

1. PRACTICE A HEALTHY LIFESTYLE

Many times, stress accumulates because we do not take care of our physical, mental, and emotional health on a regular basis. Then, when we face a crisis in one of these areas, we look for solutions to a problem we could have prevented. To live free of stress, it is important to follow these foundational good practices: exercise regularly; eat a healthy, balanced diet; get enough sleep; stay active; and engage in activities that refresh your mind, such as a favorite hobby or sport. These are natural components of life that play an important role in the prevention and reduction of stress.

One of the main answers to stress is physical rest.

---

2. KEEP EVERYTHING IN ORDER

Disorder is stressful. It does not allow you to think clearly, hinders creativity, lowers performance, and increases the time it takes to complete a task. This means that, where there's disorder, everything requires more effort, time, and energy. We must endeavor to maintain order in our emotions, thoughts, relationships, and environment, whether at home, at work, at school, or other settings. My advice for eliminating a great amount of stress at its root is to make a decision to start putting everything in good order in the various aspects of your life, including your family relationships and finances.

3. DISCONNECT FROM YOUR DAILY ROUTINE

We all follow some kind of routine as we go about life. Sometimes, we find ourselves on "automatic pilot" while completing daily tasks and fulfilling ongoing responsibilities. When we never disconnect from our routine, not even occasionally, we can fall into apathy or frustration. As our stress level rises and our creativity diminishes, we are pulled away from God's purposes. However, when we take time for a change of pace, whether to explore a new idea or place, or take a refreshing break, our mind can be recharged and our attitudes can be renewed.

This is not about neglecting our responsibilities. Each person can continue to monitor and oversee their responsibilities without allowing them to become all-consuming or impact them negatively. Every so often, I take three days off to disengage from the ministry and my everyday tasks so that I do not allow stress to build in my life.

4. GIVE GOD CONTROL

If we give control of our lives to God, He will take care of all our needs. What He has called us to do is actually His work, not ours! We must allow Him to take full charge. In this book, we have seen how people fall prey to stress because they have not surrendered their will to God. While they struggle to maintain control of their lives, they continue to carry the heavy burden of their problems. Unfortunately, God cannot help them if they do not "lay down their arms" and surrender their will. My recommendation? Make the decision immediately to surrender your will!

In the Bible, we read about a woman named Martha who tried to explain to Jesus that He had arrived late to her crisis because her brother, Lazarus, had already died. Jesus replied, *"Did I not say to you that if you would believe you would see the glory of God?"* (John 11:40). Only when Martha stopped interfering and trying to do things the way she thought they should be was the stone removed from the tomb and the one who was dead resurrected. Today, surrender your will, and you will see how God manifests His power!

5. REST IN GOD'S PEACE

Anything that does not come from God will take away our peace and cause stress. Remember that the Scriptures say,

Be anxious for nothing, but in everything by prayer and supplication, with thanksgiving, let your requests be made known to God; and the peace of God, which surpasses all understanding, will guard your hearts and minds through Christ Jesus. (Philippians 4:6–7)

We truly have a God of peace, so we do not need to live in a stressed-out state. Quite the opposite: we will have peace even in the middle of life's storms. *"We are more than conquerors through Him who loved us"* (Romans 8:37). Let us follow the example of David, who, before a decisive battle, knew how to rest in God. That is why he declared, *"The Lord, who delivered me from the paw of the lion and from the paw of the bear, He will deliver me from the hand of this Philistine"* (1 Samuel 17:37). Similarly, we can say, "The Lord has delivered me before, and I am ready to see how He will do it again."

6. LET GO OF ALL BURDENS

We need to learn to surrender all our burdens to God. As the apostle Peter advised, *"Therefore humble yourselves under the mighty hand of God, that He may exalt you in due time, casting all your care upon Him, for He cares for you"* (1 Peter 5:6–7). The prophet Isaiah declared this word from the Lord: *"Is this not the fast that I have chosen: to loose the bonds of wickedness, to undo the heavy burdens, to let the oppressed go free, and that you break every yoke?"* (Isaiah 58:6). For God to work in our lives and do the miracles we need, we must let go of our heavy burdens of oppression and cast out all anxiety. So, if you are carrying a burden you were never meant to carry, take these biblical words to heart. Do not let stress stop you from living in the peace of the Lord and receiving the blessing of the Father.

No matter what burden is causing you stress, do not carry it any longer. Let it go, right now; give it to the Lord, because He will take special care of that situation. You need to let God deal with your financial problem, illness, past failings, lack of forgiveness, and so on. Give Him that problem now! *"Be still, and know that I am God; I will be exalted among the nations, I will be exalted in the earth!"* (Psalm 46:10).

> *When we let go of our burdens, we can rest in God, knowing that He will fight our battles for us.*

7. DO NOT WORRY ABOUT TOMORROW

God's Word urges us not to anticipate bad things happening to us: *"Therefore I say to you, do not worry about your life, what you will eat or what you will drink; nor about your body, what you will put on. Is not life more than food and the body more than clothing?"* (Matthew 6:25). What we think in our minds, we will usually speak with our mouths, and finally, what we have spoken will happen. We materialize it through our thoughts and words. Job said, *"For the thing I greatly feared has come upon me, and what I dreaded has happened to me"* (Job 3:25). If you live stressed by something that causes you fear, that's what you will attract. But if you live by faith, all of God's blessings will come upon you.

> *Any mental stronghold that has not been destroyed will be like a den of stress.*

8. MEDITATE ON GOD AND HIS WORD

First, let me clarify that when I speak of "meditating," I am not referring to emptying your mind, as some groups teach. To do so is to open the door for demonic spirits or oppressions to enter your life. We must meditate on the Word of God, the Bible, which shows us the way of truth and will guide our thoughts and life. Meditating is an action similar to ruminating; it is to slowly consider an idea—to ponder it, think about it, reflect on it, and mull it over in the mind. As we meditate on God's Word, or His thoughts, we will become filled with Him, and everything in our life will change for the better. That is why, when the Lord spoke to Joshua to guide His people to occupy the promised land, He said, *"This Book of the Law shall not depart from your mouth, but you shall meditate in it day and night, that you may observe to do according to all that is written in it. For then you will make your way prosperous, and then you will have good success"* (Joshua 1:8).

Meditating on the Word also makes it easier for us to hear the voice of God in our spirit. When we get used to meditating on God's Word, the next thing that will come is revelation, or a deep understanding by the Spirit of the truths we are reading. Keep in mind that it is not enough just to meditate. We must remain in the Word on which we are meditating. This means that we must act in accordance with what it says. *"Be doers of the word, and not hearers only, deceiving yourselves"* (James 1:22).

9. SEEK INNER HEALING AND DELIVERANCE

If you find that after following the previous tips, you still cannot live free of stress, there may be a malignant spiritual influence at work from which you need to be freed. Look for a church that believes in the complete work of Jesus on the cross and ministers it. Jesus paid a high price for our freedom, and the work of the cross includes inner healing and deliverance. Sometimes we require the help of a mature believer who can minister to us and break the spiritual bondages that have come upon us and are hurting us, so that we can walk in the freedom of Christ. Today is the day the Lord wants to heal your heart and deliver you! He is waiting for you with open arms.

10. MAINTAIN A CONTINUOUS RELATIONSHIP WITH JESUS CHRIST

Dear reader, if you are living with unrelenting stress and do not know how to ask God to take away your burdens, I want to invite you to enter into a relationship with Jesus Christ by receiving Him into your heart. Living without stress requires an ongoing relationship with Him that includes prayer and reading the Word. If you have not yet recognized Jesus as your Lord and Savior, please say this prayer aloud:

Heavenly Father, I acknowledge that I am a sinner and that my sin separates me from You. I believe that Jesus died on the cross for my sins and that You raised Him from the dead. I repent of all my sins and voluntarily confess Jesus as my Lord and Savior. I renounce all covenants with the world, all worldly thinking and behavior; with the desires of my flesh, every desire that is contrary to Your will; and with the devil. Instead, I make a covenant with Jesus to love and follow Him. I ask Jesus to enter my heart and change my life. If I were to die today, I know that I would be in Your arms, to live with You forever. Amen!

TRUE STORIES OF OVERCOMING OPPRESSIVE STRESS

Major League Transformation

Carlos Zambrano is a well-known Major League Baseball player in the United States who played for both the Chicago Cubs and the Miami Marlins. He is remembered for his great successes as a pitcher. Despite growing up in a Christian home in his native Venezuela, he turned away from God until he lived through a season of intense pressure from which only God could rescue him.

Despite my having sunken into sin, God always showed me His unconditional love. I remember a day in Guatemala when I seemed to be on the verge of death. I suddenly began to feel dizzy and to have an irregular heartbeat, and my blood pressure kept fluctuating. Doctors from Venezuela and Chicago immediately saw me and kept me connected to heart monitors the whole day, but they did not find anything wrong with me. I was then rushed to a hospital in Chicago so I could be seen by the team doctor, but he did not find anything wrong either. However, I was not okay and literally lived in a desperate state, under enormous stress.

I returned to Venezuela, where I went to see my personal doctor, a brother in Christ who understands both the medical and spiritual side of things, and it was then that I was able to understand what was happening to me. He told me, "Carlos, we've done all the tests, and there is nothing wrong physically. What you have is spiritual, my friend. God is calling you, and He is giving you a chance."

These words initiated a transformation that would lead me to seek God and start learning about His kingdom. I made the best and biggest decision I have made in my life, better than when I decided to sign my contract with the Chicago Cubs and bigger than when I decided to get married. It was the decision to die to self in order to allow Christ to live in me. Before making that decision, I had focused on material things and vanities, but I lived without peace. I was always angry and in trouble. However, when this change occurred, the offenses or hurts other people committed against me no longer affected me, because now I knew that Christ is the one who fights for me. There is nothing more beautiful than being led by Him and resting in His presence. Nothing compares to the love of God.

Currently, I live in Miami; my family is happy, and I have peace in my heart and in my spirit, knowing that God directs my life. Never again have I felt the sensation that I was dying, or the palpitations or fainting, because I have an intimate and permanent relationship with God and He directs my life. I can say that, in the midst of any situation, I rest in God. By His grace, after being trained at King Jesus church in Miami, under the fatherhood of Apostle Guillermo Maldonado, I am fulfilling the pastoral call that God placed in my heart.

Athlete of Faith

Dayana is an American-Canadian athlete who experienced depression as a child. She sought love and recognition through sports, but only God could give her what her heart needed.

From an early age, I had to deal with poverty and all kinds of shortcomings, as well as an immense emptiness inside me. My stepfather was violent with my mother and me, and he abused me. I grew up with a lot of depression and struggled with my self-esteem. I did not know what to believe because although my family went to church, I also practiced voodoo. Due to my stepfather's abuse, I felt empty and without love. That's why I started to rebel, until I left home.

I began looking for God because I knew that He had answered my prayers before. However, at nineteen, I fell into an abusive relationship that, in time, ended in divorce. After much despair, I did not know where to go in search of love, so I began to idolize my own body and make appearances in bodybuilding shows. Soon, I felt that I had found my purpose in life. I became well-known in that field, with my picture appearing in magazines. I earned money for presentations, and I even won the Ms. Olympia award.

I thought that the fitness world was giving my life purpose, but it did not satisfy me. I was so focused on bodybuilding that I was getting farther and farther away from God. Only when I understood that I had to return to His arms did I begin to make my way back to Him. God began to free me from the depression and disappointments of the past. I felt that my life had found new meaning in Him. Today, I am a retired athlete, but nothing that I achieved in the past can compare to the freedom God has given me. He opened a door for me to have my own radio program called *Fitness and Faith*. Now I know that there is much more of God to come, and that fills me with joy.

Today, Dayana is free of depression. She leads a healthy life because she lives in the peace of Christ and maintains an intimate and continuous relationship with Him. For you, the solution to filling the void in your heart, being loved, and finding a purpose in life is the same. God is just waiting for you to surrender to Him so He can heal you and bless you with stress-free living.

ABOUT THE AUTHOR

Apostle Guillermo Maldonado is the senior pastor and founder of King Jesus International Ministry (Ministerio Internacional El Rey Jesus) in Miami, Florida, a multicultural church considered to be one of the fastest growing in the United States. King Jesus Ministry, whose foundation is built upon the Word of God, prayer, and worship, currently has a membership of nearly seventeen thousand. Apostle Maldonado is a spiritual father to more than 350 churches in 50 countries throughout the United States, Latin America, Europe, Africa, Asia, and New Zealand, which form the Supernatural Global Network, representing over six hundred thousand people. He is also the founder of the University of the Supernatural Ministry (USM). The building of kingdom leaders and the visible manifestations of God's supernatural power distinguish the ministry as the number of its members constantly multiplies.

A national best-selling author, Apostle Maldonado has written over fifty books and manuals, many of which have been translated into other languages. His books with Whitaker House include *Breakthrough Prayer*, *Breakthrough Fast*, *How to Walk in the Supernatural Power of God*, *The Glory of God*, *The Kingdom of Power*, *Supernatural Transformation*, *Supernatural Deliverance*, and *Divine Encounter with the Holy Spirit*, all of which are available in both English and Spanish. In addition, he preaches the message of Jesus Christ and His redemptive power on his international television program, *The Supernatural Now* (*Lo sobrenatural ahora*), which airs on TBN, Daystar, the Church Channel, and fifty other networks, with a potential outreach and impact to more than two billion people around the world.

Apostle Maldonado has a doctorate in Christian counseling from Vision International University and a master's degree in practical theology from Oral Roberts University. He resides in Miami, Florida, with his wife and ministry partner, Ana, and their two sons, Bryan and Ronald.